imagine

A NIGHT

imagi

paintings by ROB GONSALVES

text by SARAH L. THOMSON

ne

A
NIGHT

a byron preiss visual publications, inc. book

atheneum books for young readers

NEW YORK   LONDON   TORONTO   SYDNEY   SINGAPORE

imagine a night...

...when snow white sheets

grow crisp and cold,

and someone whispers,

"Follow me."

imagine a night...

...when you can't sleep,

and so you jump

high enough to soar

over a quilt of fields and forests.

imagine a night...

...when a whistle echoes

from an empty hall,

and a voice calls, "All aboard!"

No ticket needed

to travel

to a place no one has seen.

imagine a night...

...when—Listen!—you can hear
a farmer play his fields to sleep,
a lullaby for leaf and stem
and dreaming root.

imagine a night...

...when the darkness

of meadow and lake

feels too quiet and deep,

and so you cut and stitch a city

from the starry sky.

imagine a night...

...when drifts of moonlight

take on shape and form,

and you look over your shoulder

to find you're not alone.

imagine a night...

...when you might find

that gravity

doesn't work

quite as you expected.

imagine a night...

...when candlelight rises

on butterfly wings

to greet the lonely stars.

imagine a night...

...when moonlight spills

across the water

to make a path

for the lightest feet.

imagine a night...

...when velvet darkness hangs

at every window,

so that our dreams

will never end.

imagine a night...

...when a new partner

joins the stately dance

of moon around Earth

and Earth around sun.

imagine a night...

...when you take

just one last ride;

beneath you, the hill grows steep

and your wheels

grow wings.

imagine a night...

...when the space between words

becomes like the space

between trees:

wide enough

to wander in.

imagine a night...

. . . when a snowfall

tucks you in

and the evening star

kisses you asleep.

Imagine . . . tonight.

This book was inspired by the following paintings,
which led the writer to imagine . . .

In the Aurora

Candlelit Cloister

Cold Comfort

Bedtime Aviation

House by the Railroad

Listening Fields

A Change of Scenery

Medieval Moonlight

With love to Lise,
my partner in the magical dance
—R. G.

To Julian—always imagine
—S. L. T.

Nocturnal Cycling

Fallen Stars

Ladies of the Lake

Astral Projections

New Moon Eclipsed

Coasting

Woods Within

White Blanket

To learn more about Rob Gonsalves' work, or to find his work in a gallery near you, please visit www.discoverygalleries.com
or the Discovery Gallery at 4840 Bethesda Avenue, Bethesda, Maryland 20814, (301) 913-9199.

Atheneum Books for Young Readers
An imprint of Simon & Schuster Children's Publishing Division
1230 Avenue of the Americas
New York, New York 10020
Copyright © 2003 by Rob Gonsalves and Byron Preiss Visual Publications, Inc.
Text and illustrations copyright © 2003 by Rob Gonsalves
All rights reserved, including the right of reproduction in whole or in part in any form.
Book design by Ann Bobco and Abelardo Martínez
The text of this book is set in Centaur.
The illustrations are rendered in acrylics.
Manufactured in China
First Edition

10 9 8 7 6 5 4 3 2 1
Library of Congress Cataloging-in-Publication Data
Gonsalves, Rob.
Imagine a night / illustrated by Rob Gonsalves.
p.   cm.
Summary: Presents a night when imagination takes over and gravity does not work
quite as expected.
ISBN 0-689-85218-5
[1. Night—Fiction. 2. Imagination—Fiction. 3. Snow—Fiction.
4. Bedtime—Fiction.] I. Gonsalves, Rob, ill. II. Title.
PZ7 .T3815 Im 2003
[E]—dc21   2002010718